Transport

Le transport

ler trons-*paw*

Illustrated by Clare Beaton

Illustré par Clare Beaton

b small publishing

bicycle

la bicyclette

lah bee-see-*klet*

car

la voiture

lah vwot-*yure*

lorry

le camion

ler camee-*oh*

boat

le bateau

ler bat-*oh*

bus

l'autobus

low-toh-*boos*

fire engine

le camion de pompiers

ler camee-*oh* der pompee-*eh*

motorbike

la moto

lah moh-*toh*

tractor

le tracteur

ler tract-err

digger

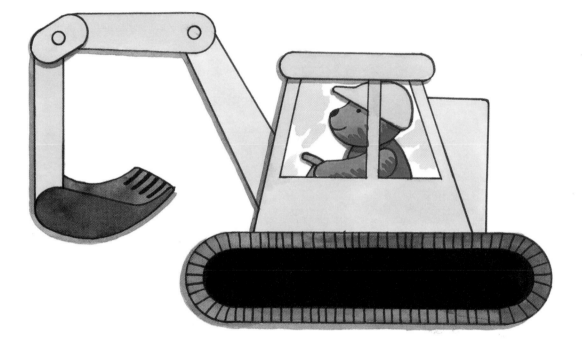

la pelleteuse

lah pellet-*ers*

aeroplane

l'avion

lavee-*oh*

train

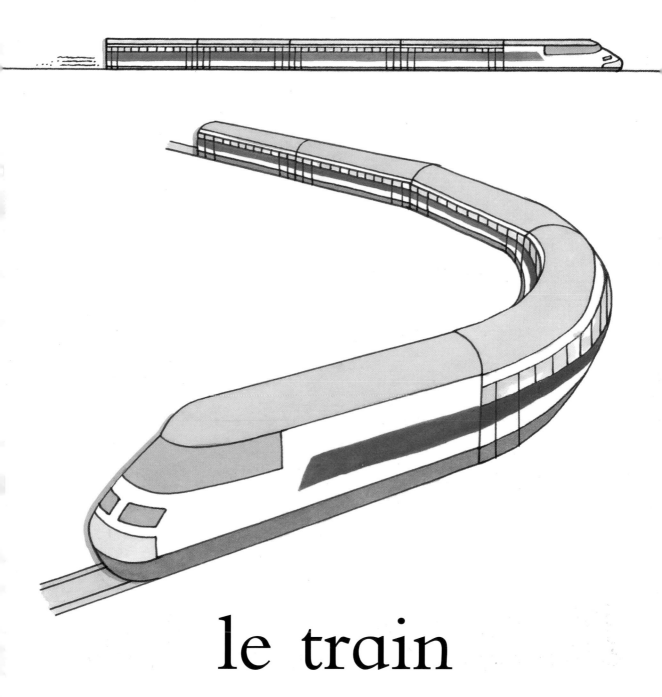

le train

ler trah

A simple guide to pronouncing the French words

- Read this guide as naturally as possible, as if it were standard British English.
- Put stress on the letters in *italics* e.g. lah vwot-*yure*
- Don't roll the r at the end of the word, e.g. in the French word le (the): ler.

la bicyclette	lah bee-see-*klet*	**bicycle**
la voiture	lah vwot-*yure*	**car**
le camion	ler camee-*oh*	**lorry**
le bateau	ler bat-*oh*	**boat**
l'autobus	low-toh-*boos*	**bus**
le camion de pompiers	ler camee-*oh* der pompee-*eh*	**fire engine**
la moto	lah moh-*toh*	**motorbike**
le tracteur	ler tract-*err*	**tractor**
la pelleteuse	lah pellet-*ers*	**digger**
l'avion	lavee-*oh*	**aeroplane**
le train	ler trah	**train**

Published by b small publishing

The Book Shed, 36 Leyborne Park, Kew, Richmond, Surrey, TW9 3HA, UK

www.bsmall.co.uk

© b small publishing, 2002 and 2008 (new cover)

4 5 6

All rights reserved.

Printed in China by WKT Company Ltd.

ISBN-13: 978-1-902915-68-5 (UK paperback)

Cataloguing-in-Publication Data:

A catalogue record for this book is available from the British Library